POEMS

about 101 topics

Scottie Awesome Powers

About the Author

I currently live in Mchenry, Illinois. Happily married to my beautiful wife Hannah. We have one child so far; our little boy Bruce is 1 year old now. I first grew up in Midlothian, Illinois then moved to Buffalo Grove. Then, when my mom got married, I transferred from Stevenson High School to Waukegan High School. I graduated with high honors. For college, I got my associate's Degree in Arts from the College of Lake County.

I work from home as a customer service representative in the evenings. I worked in the restaurant industry for many years all around the area. I am known as the waiter poet.

I started writing poetry in High School then took college creative writing courses. After schooling, I continued to write poetry, short stories, and a few movie scripts and I recorded a few songs too. I got serious about my poetry performing at open mic shows in Chicago. I would go to Roger's Park once a week to an open mic show sponsored by In One Ear. They've been hosting performers since the 90's. I would travel all over the area to do open mic shows wherever I could find a good gig, and In One Ear is the best. I went every week for 2-3 years to really hone in on my craft.

I am a Christian, raised Catholic. My beliefs are not always your standard, but I hope they align with the truth. I speak my mind, and I don't hold anything back. I am the type of guy who puts everything out there. Honesty is a virtue I hope you appreciate. Thank you for reading.

Dedication

This book is dedicated to my moms, plural. My Mom, my mother, who gave birth to me, Jean Denam. She went to heaven on 4/17/2022, Easter Sunday, between 3 am and 4 am, the angel hour. My mother-in-law Connie Anderson, also called MorMor, which is Swedish for Grandma. My Grandma, Judith Powers, may not be able to read it now(dementia), but I know she is proud of me. My Stepmother, Karyn Schronski because I know she loves me very much. My two other moms, my Aunt Kathie Elliott and my Aunt Linda Purtell know how important they are to me. And last but not least, my wife, Hannah Powers, who is mom to our son Bruce.

Also, thank you to all my fans and all the people who have supported me over the years. It has been a long time in the making to have my first published book. This epic masterpiece was constructed in a specific way for a specific purpose, without any swears, for all adults to enjoy.

Introduction

I would like to quickly explain the structure behind this book and its purpose. People know I'm a poet. I was gifted a writer's prompt book with many topics to write about with blank pages. On the side of each page, for each topic, are 8-word associations to help you get started. I didn't choose these words; they were right there on the side of the page. I took it as a challenge to incorporate these 8 words into each poem. For each subject, I would use all 8 words for that subject, in the most creative way I could while still maintaining cohesion in a poem and, of course, making it me.

The goal of my poetry is to open your mind and make you think/question your beliefs. I will make you laugh, smile, cry, get angry. I hope I make you feel every emotion while going through the different subjects in this book with me. I am hoping each line is unpredictable to you but yet somehow feels familiar. A lot of pop culture references, as well as some inside jokes. Some things will be very clear to understand, while others will make absolutely no sense to some people. I reference a lot of my favorite things while discussing some extreme personal issues. I am different; I am awesome, and you are awesome, too, for giving me a chance. Read it straight through, and bounce around to your favorite subjects. Nothing is quite as it seems. I hope you enjoy!

Contents

WRITE A POEM ABOUT

The Ocean

First sun

Eyes open, alleviate bowels, brush teeth, drink water

Deep breathes, positive thoughts

Meditation, yoga, journal, breakfast

Outside the ocean *billows*, surf beckons

Wash the board, 6am beat the *tide*

The dawn patrol twin fin gets to hang ten

Early bird gets the worm

Rise and shine, *brine* and grind

Last night's moon, today's *wave*

Wind *current* in *flux*

Offing unclear

Appears nuts

Scottie P's in the suit

Billows – Deep – Brine – Offing – Wave – Flux – Tide – Current

WRITE A POEM ABOUT

Parents

God's bridge to eternal life

My Mother is in Heaven

Jesus finally got his bride

I won't be able to dance with her at my wedding

She has her brother and her father to party with now

I pray she is proud of me

Now starting my own family

My *childhood*, us against the world

My *mother*, my brother, and I

No *father* to discipline

Surrounded by a community

Influencing the wrong *upbringing*

Mom did her best

To *nurture*, love, protect

A *guardian* against all threats

She was a *teacher* of scripture to children

She ran a counseling group D. A.

I think she would want my grief and depression to go away

I can honor her having a strong moral integrity

Spiritually spreading the good message

No false *idol* worship

Following my passion

Confidently pursuing my dreams

Organizing priorities

Handling my responsibilities

She only wanted me to be fulfilled and happy

Thank you Mom, you did it, I am

And I will be, until I see you again

When it's my time to cross God's bridge

Guardian – Idol – Nurture – Mother – Father – Childhood – Upbringing –
Teacher

WRITE A POEM ABOUT

The Past

Flashback picture the *memory*

Tell the story

Adlib facts, un-exaggerate straight fate

In a *distant* land, a galaxy far, far away

Right here, right there

The night before, set to celebrate Easter

I was at her house

I was checking in our her, I didn't like what I saw

I left anyway thinking it would all be okay

She went to the hospital

I knew she needed fluids and monitoring

They told me she passed early in the morning

A week for the funeral

Reality is *bygone*

Piece together a *memoir* to speak

Large gathering for the *remembrance* of the tremendous hero

Weak knees needed courage to stand at the podium

Tears flooded the parlor

Many friends told tales of *long ago*

I gave each person a moment

Touched by an angel

At the gates of heaven, she is a greeter

For now, process 5 stages

Possession allocation, find the *antiquity*

Our family *history*

We overcame all tragedies

Pride for your honor

Decision, discussions, Dad is due too

True bonds, true colors, success, failure

The future is our potential

The past is over

But will always be a part of us

Memory – Distant – History – Remembrance – Antiquity – Memoir – Bygone – Long ago

WRITE A POEM ABOUT

The Future

January 1ˢᵗ, a great day to discuss the future

My wife and I plan the *potential* baby, to nurture

It is our *destiny* to be parents

We *foresee* a healthy pregnancy

No sleep, crying, dirty diapers

Breast-feeding in middle of the night

Super elated moments, and scary low's

Lost patience is *imminent*

Pacifiers are binky's, bottles are baba's

Great grandpa is Boppa, and grandma is Mormor

My Mom is Nana Jean in heaven

I *hope* my child understands why we visit her grave every Easter

Teach him or her about our history

Know where you're from to get where you're going

Take advantage of every good *opportunity*

Have conviction to seal the covenant

The *prophesy* was written

My baby will become the new patriarch of the family

Leading the next generation

To the promised land, a grand kingdom

My *fate* to be the dad of the next great man or woman

Be a great father to all the children

My identity is linked to my destiny

Thoughts, words, actions, habits, character

I will create for myself and my family

An amazing future

Destiny – Hope – Potential – Imminent – Opportunity – Fate – Foresee –
Prophesy

WRITE A POEM ABOUT

A Storm

Gerry is a good guy

He was taking Paxil and Lexapro

He managed his anxiety pharmaceutically

There was a flood

A *raging* storm, *tempestuous*

The whole block went under water 6 feet deep

Gerry used a canoe boating buckets and sand bags

In an attempt to salvage his parent's crib

The *wrath* of *squall*

Like a *gale* of smoke left by Wil. E. Coyote

Friends dashed fast in a rush to help

Bricks were used like rulers measuring the rising water level

Hustle, bustle, and muscle saved the day

After a month, the water still laid

Billy thought it would be a great idea to grab his motorbike and
race

Slipped, flipped, and crashed his bike into an electric pole

It was a bad accident

Billy didn't make it

Funeral at Kolssak Funeral Home

Tim, Gerry's friend and neighbor, was minding his business, at home alone, using his computer

Earlier in the evening, he had been complaining of a headache but paid no attention to it

He went out to a bar, had a few drinks

Came back home, to his pc, had an aneurysm

Tim didn't make it

Funeral at Kolssak Funeral Home

It was only days after Billy died at the opposite end of the same street

3 weeks later, Gerry's mom didn't awake from her sleep

In the morning, her husband, went to his job, when he came home in the afternoon, she was cold

She went to heaven from her bed, the cops had no explanation

Gerry's mom didn't make it

Funeral at Kolssak Funeral Home

3 of his closest peeps

Ripped from the world

Can you imagination a *roaring* storm taking so much

A devastating amount of pain from the *blustering* amount of rain

I couldn't blame Gerry for wanting to shoot himself

Upset, fumbling with his gun

He was mumbling to himself on the couch

I did shit my pants when he pointed the gun at me

I came out of the bathroom too suddenly

It was an accident, he wasn't in his right mind

Glad he didn't *blast* either of us

His sister sent him to the psych ward for help

I forgive my friend that went on a bend

Gerry can always depend on me

Within a month, his whole life was swallowed up

All surrounding a freaky storm

WRITE A POEM ABOUT

Colors

Ice-T was a nightmare walking, psychopath talking

Before he became law and order

Brilliance is relative

Deciphering light from *shade*

Beauty is in the eye of the beholder

Photograph the moment in a mental picture

Also, on an I-phone

The *scarlet* sunset with *vermillion* hue

Her *complexion* radiated

Each *pigment* of skin glistening like a diamond

The water reflected images of free spirits

Catching glimpses of each individual aura

Her's pink, his *cobalt*

The *tincture* of felicity softened his heart

Tripled its size

The aura's mixed light combined the colors

The scene florescent orange

Passionate sex on the beach

We drank twisted Arnold Palmer's

3 each

Pigment - Shade – Tincture – Complexion – Scarlet – Cobalt – Brilliance – Vermillion

WRITE A POEM ABOUT

First Love

Love comes first

First thing is love

First the day is lovely

I *relish* the morning quiet

Gratitude attitude

Thank you for this breathe

Walk the dog, feed the cat

Kiss my wife

Routine- breakfast, journal, yoga

Order opposite doubts

Affirm action

Blaze the *flame*

Passion ignites

Pursue the truth

Overcoming *youth* trauma

Discipline *yearning*

Lessons learned

Opportunity knocking

Devotion, duty to my family

Cherishing each moment un-alone

Enchantment on her finger

Faith on my sleeve

Confidence is protection from evil

Come back home

Tenderness on the table

Comfort in-between the sheets

Séances, habitual mystical rituals

Strong belief in supernatural power

Holy matrimony, wedding vows

Beginning, end

Alpha, Omega

First love, last love

Forever love

Tenderness – Relish – Flame – Yearning – Cherishing – Passion –
Enchantment – Youth

WRITE A POEM ABOUT

Kisses

Mucho kisses for Mrs. Powers

My honey, babe, sweetheart

My love

Happy wife, happy life

I give all

Thought, emotion, *passion*

Actions toward our benevolence

You lead by example

I will always choose you

When we *embrace*, I *caress* your soul

Sexy, *wet lips*, gorgeous eyes, *warm* touch

I will never let go

The ring is the *clasp*

The ceremony honored Him

For better or worse

Rain, hail, sleet, snow, wind

You perform under all conditions

You have incredible stamina

To kiss for hours

In bed *cheek* to cheek

A teacher, trainer

I learned how to be more peaceful

A super woman

I wonder how I got to be so lucky

You choose me to be your eternal partner

Your husband Mr. Powers

WRITE A POEM ABOUT

Treasure

Smothering tithe

An extorsion of treasure

The pleasure of hoarding incredible *wealth*

Vision a golden river

Dipping my hands in, pulling out large bars

An *abundance* of cash

Imagine an immaculate *fortune*

Daydream of owning fancy cars

High fashion clothes

Rare jewels, *precious* metals

Mandalorian armor

Provide market *value*

Ill skills get paid

Cache the *trove*

Haters gonna hate

Trove – Precious – Rare – Wealth – Value – Abundance – Fortune – Cache

WRITE A POEM ABOUT

Children

We were going to have a baby

My girlfriend got pregnant

I married her, but not for that reason

I love my wife with all my heart

Our life is good, we are happy

Building a family

We want *kids*

Common goals

Raising our own *little foundling*

We know God has a plan

She had a miscarriage

I could have let that get me totally depressed, but I didn't

I had to be strong for her

A creature passed through her body

Came from heaven, then went back

She is buried in the garden

Aurora Zoe

The *offspring* was in the womb, only 8 weeks

We dreamed of her future

We would grow, learn, *play* together

I could see her with the other *youngsters*

Leading the *youth* to the truth

School, sports, art, philosophy, music

A *toddler* with toys, imagining, adventuring

At the Christmas party, opening presents with cousins

My wife and I visualized riding rides at carnivals, taking family vacations

Teaching her about the beauty and wonders of the world

The miracle of life

We endured the grief of death

Everything comes full circle

A year and a half later, we were blessed to be pregnant with her brother

Toddler – Play – Offspring – Kids – Little – Foundling – Youngsters – Youth

WRITE A POEM ABOUT

A Mystery

Hidden theme

A labyrinth to reveal neverland

What a *conundrum,* the sadness *enigma*

Painful *quandary*- lose 5 of your life or discard a card

Avoid therapy; quite a *pickle* Rick

Ru appalled the *charade* of bad drag racing

His lust for sluts his crutch- a whore *crux*

Trading places in blue suede shoes

Get out of your head, wear ear dampeners

Take control of other's minds gamer

You can't *baffle* me- unreal engine

For more than a fortnite. no ghosts at this haunted mansion

Uncanny- he is the android

Real genius builds lasers

Stick a recording transmitter underneath Jessie's bed

I need to hear who Kelly will choose for the dance

Clear the streets when Omar starts whistling

Scarface say hello to my little friend

A crow left of the murder she wrote

I write sins not tragedies

Bring the noise Terminator X

In *puzzlement*, the renegade drove by the fork in the road and went straight

Past 3 billboards in Ebbing, Missouri

In reverse, memento- a black mirror

Use any object as a weapon hitman

Perfect dark for a golden eye

Grand theft auto, gone in 60 seconds

Tony Starks did not survive

Rise of the Ghostface Killah

Quick Doc, take the DeLorean back to the future

Conundrum – Pickle – Quandary – Crux – Enigma – Puzzlement –
Charade – Baffle

WRITE A POEM ABOUT

A Voice

You seem to kick when I talk

You recognize my voice

I had a right to remain silent

I chose to *holler*

Now, I'm in the spotlight

Noise with cohesion

That's my goal

Advice from a respected mentor

Maybe even hero

Sheild you from evil

Lead by example

Protect the precious vessel your soul resides in

Feed the *instinct* for strength

Cut *husky*, large physical frame

Brain with phenomenal computation

My son, the miracle

Quantum leap of faith

Whisper truths throughout your youth

Avoid subliminal audio

Watch out for criminals

Keep your friends close and your enemies closer

Millions of little proverbs

Sultry injected into the sub-*conscience*

Speaking in *soft* tones

Growth from birth to my end

A *murmur* from Mormor

Parental figure recognition

Your birth cry was music to my ears

Murmur – Whisper – Holler – Soft – Husky – Sultry – Conscience – Instinct

WRITE A POEM ABOUT

Eternity

I know you're there

Perpetual overwatching

Without judgement

Humbly proud

Everlasting love

Reach inside, I can always touch

I can see your eyes when I close mine

Smile at the thought of your smile

Feel the grace of your warm embrace

Endless comfort

An angel supports us

Never met your grandson

I know you know his face

Protect him like a babysitter from Heaven

Named after your dad

Powers for *infinity*

Passing down a legacy

Proving *immortality* is not a fallacy

Beyond earth, universe, galaxy

The electron connection phenomenon

Providing *eon* ion energy

Eliminate wiring *lasting* electricity

Spiritual bond transcends this realm

Painting the father, I will become

The *future* is a large empty canvas

You shaped my brush

I can never lose the truth

You are a part of my heart for eternity Mom

Infinity – Everlasting – Perpetual – Endless – Future – Immortality – Eon –
Lasting

WRITE A POEM ABOUT

Science Fiction

Invasion of the killer-tomatoes

Mars attacks

Explore the infinite cosmos

I robot ideas

Every *alien* is a *humanoid*

The matrix steals life energy

People turned into batteries

Soul sucking, 9 to 5, gears in the machine

Heroes and villains

The universal story

Power versus peace

An unimaginable utopia

In a *galaxy* far, far away

Light exposure radioactive decay

A star trek, *space* is the final frontier

Rocket science, SpaceX rockets to the future

Dinosaurs roamed the center of the planet, Pangia

The tide always faces the moon, the oceans turn

Current winds fluctuate temperatures

Time springs forward, and later falls back

Measurement zone Celsius or metric

Parallel universes, wormholes or flumes

Inclusion illusion, seclusion *abduction*

Culture killed spirit broken

Get over the delusion one day it all has to end

What always will be, has always been

*Space – Alien – Explore – Abduction – Invasion – Future – Humanoid –
Galaxy*

Intelligence

Wu is for the children

Wisdom is choosing the right future

Mind over matter

I learned about the struggle from hip-hop, from rappers

The RZA is the Abbot

Wu-Tang is the greatest rap group of all time

Originally 9 members, 4 chambers of the heart, the first album- 36 chambers

Business, branding, marketing, fashion

Passionate message

A purpose to bring good to the hood

Raise awareness promoting personal progress

Real life superheroes with cool aliases

Dirt McGirt, Johnny Blaze, Tony Starks

Creative *brilliance, shrewd* competitors

Swinging liquid swords while killer bees swarm attacking a broken system, extracting cream-like honey

Helped *discern* reality from dream

Encouraged to read

Learned to be *literate* listening to Wu-Tang

Gained *brains, insight* into all subjects

Mathematics, science, religion

Hearing the music, feeling the beats

Through the lyrics, *sense* the struggle of the streets

A telescope into my country

Microscope view of the problems of the projects

Wu conquest project how we all want to act

The main topic-

Imagine a better future for all of us

Use our intelligence, grow as a group

Wu is for the children

Insight – Literate – Shrewd – Brains – Discern – Mind – Brilliance – Sense

WRITE A POEM ABOUT

The Universe

The universe never lied

The teachers did, the preachers did

About *creation*, about aliens

Concepts of the *cosmos* dictated by ignorant brainwashed zombies

Following propagated book manuals

Government texts, school budgets, test prep

In *totality*, my theory of everything

The *infinite* is unfathomable

Metaphysical gravity, fall into orbits of habits

We connect internally, frequencies flow like a stream, according to
the parameters of the container

The discovery of neural kinetics

Applicable to the big bang

Entire lives pass before our eyes

Unlimited do-overs, reversible paths

Crash into the *vast* nothingness

The happy place, the good place

Space is the expansion of dark matter

Organized options for the multi-verse

In *relativity*, the decision for us is limited

Immense pleasure or pain

A pinch to wake up

Instant innocuous ending

WRITE A POEM ABOUT

A Stranger

Friend or foe yo state your biz

A hard knock, life's at the door

Jehovah's witnesses

Christ will save your soul

Sojourner of flesh

The Devil is a welcome *guest* in the immoral home

Sin is celebrated, evil is encouraged

The *visitor* ventured into the *mysterious* residence

A *newcomer* to horror

Before long he beat women, kidnapped children, stole from the
poor

Once a *migrant* destined for heaven

Groomed down another path

Fell off the stairway

An *acquaintance* to Death himself

Mr. President of Hell

Evil is a stranger in the night

Your best friend in the middle of a fight

Fear released as rage

Anxiety on stage

The enemy of my enemy is my friend

The internal eternal struggle

Showing empathy or taking advantage

Friend or foe – Sojourner – Mysterious – Guest – Newcomer – Migrant –
Visitor – Acquaintance

WRITE A POEM ABOUT

Angels

They say only angels die on Easter Sunday

Hi, my name is Apples

I am a long-haired Maine coon

I just turned 23 years old

(ppssss that's like 95 in cat years)

Let me tell you my life story

I am a total momma's boy

I came to be in her possession through a friend

I had nowhere to go, she took me in

She is just that kind of person, a good Christian

My *guardian* would feed me every morning

She refreshed the place I did my bowel business

(ppssss she cleaned the kitty litter)

I started growing and became a strong creature

She helped me develop my *spirit*

We would play, a stick had a string, I tried pounce and clutch

But the mouse at the end of it was always just out of my touch

A small red light would be on the floor, then all of a sudden jump
to the wall, and then to the chair, and then the dresser

I couldn't follow it fast enough

I wore costumes and she posted pictures on Facebook of my
beautiful long fur

I love *being* the center of attention

We have a large family, three guys come around all the time, I think
they are Mommy's grown sons

The man of the house, Papi, takes care of the dog, Trinity

Lots of aunts, uncles, and cousins

When really large parties arrive, I usually hide

After all I'm only 1 foot tall

Each evening, during sleep, we *ascend* into the *ethereal*

(ppssss that means our dreams)

I sleep on top of Mommy

We experience *heavenly* rest

I had a vision one time of a *seraph*

Next, Mommy became a Nana

One of the boys had a boy

She would babysit the kid

I would participate in the play

We had so much fun learning and growing every day

Years go by, the baby gets bigger, I get older, Momma does too

She doesn't take care of him anymore

Sometimes I think she has the flu

Sometimes she spends a few days away, they say, she was at the hospital

I know she wears a beeper, for her diabetes, but I don't know what that means

Two days after Good Friday 2022

My Mommy didn't wake up in the morning

She ascended into Heaven, and she wouldn't be coming back

I was very sad, I stayed in bed almost wishing I was dead too

Then one of the men

(ppssss one of Mommy's grown boys)

Snatched me up, put me in my carrier and carried me to his car

We drove to his home which was very, very far

There I saw his wife and his dog

I had met the pooch before but that didn't mean we got along

It took awhile for us to become buddies

You know I won't let no doggie let me feel less than amazing

My Mommy taught me to believe in myself

Now I have a new family, a renewed love

Soon the wife of the home will be a new Mommy

(ppssss I had a vision of a *cherub*)

I will watch over the baby just like she taught me

Thank you to the angel for all the lessons

I am blessed, family is sacred, I lived a great life

Soon I will join Mommy, in Heaven

WRITE A POEM ABOUT

Blessings

Thanks be to God

Blessed for the *gifts*

Tease the intellect, mind confection

Clever connection, beasty *benediction*

The Priest did *bestow grace*

Boom, boom, *boon* abundance

The luckiest man on Earth

I have everything I ever wanted

Not just *luck* could buck the muck I was stuck in

Faith in a higher power and self-help books

Affirmations increased the energy

Meditating raised the frequency

Life is an endless *bounty* of joy

Optimism into belief

From fear to love

Fair, creative exchange

Support, encouragement, trust

A shield protects us

The light guides us

The spirit within tethered to Him

Every morning, we sing

WRITE A POEM ABOUT

Innocence

A child is born

Tabula rasa- a *clean* slate

An angel touches its upper lip

Past lives forgotten

We are all born free

The *lamb* of God, made of stars

Start with *virtue*

Instinct of empathy, exhibit *temperance*

Impeccable beauty, art, *artless*

Undeveloped, limitless

Indestructible *modesty*

No wrong baby, wrong parent

Teach *decency* lead by example

Careful caresses, supple kisses

Never mistake my kindness for a weakness

I'm not that innocent

Gregorius personality

Mess with my kid

Be sure I'm coming after you

Protecting the innocent, everything I believe in

Virtue – Clean – Lamb – Impeccable – Artless – Modesty – Decency - Temperance

Brotherhood

There is not to reason why, there is but to do and die

Fubar, *steadfast* for survival

I don't take orders anymore

Comradeship in war against corporations

Not *loyal* to any company

In the *fraternity* of the service field

Waiter, warehouse, retail

Brick and mortar marginalized

Amazon, Temu, Ebay

Drones deliver merchandise in the mail

Increased insurance premiums

The median income cannot afford a home

Negotiate inches

In *fellowship* with bargainers

A *partner* to outsiders

Solidarity for our views

Every day everyone is focusing

Hustling, bustling, destroying themselves

We need relaxation, patience, empathy

More *unity* in our community

Today we travel virtually; work remotely

Spam emails, scam calls

I'm looking for a brotherhood to do good

Kindness, compassion, courtesy, respect

After Covid, we were supposed to learn a lesson

I'm afraid we didn't

Only action in our control is to fight the system

Instead of fighting amongst our brothers

WRITE A POEM ABOUT

Smiles

Many styles of smiles

But you can't force it

Lips smirk too tight

If the feeling isn't right

Find *delight*, hormones ignite

Chemicals blast, *amusement-* gas

I *laugh*, you laugh, we all laugh

I scream, you scream, we all scream

A *beam* of happiness

Simple little *grin*

The *dimple* wins the women

Grin – Laugh – Amusement – Delight – Smirk – Beam – Dimple – Lips

WRITE A POEM ABOUT

Clouds

Where information is stored

Puff, puff, pass

Blow out the *mist*

I.T. technical support

Reset the charcoal on the hookah

The bonfire *billow*

Kids imagine dragons

Santa's beard, an elephant

Look at a cumulonimbus

The *thunderhead* of mythology

Angels *swarm* from the *nebulous*

A *cumulous* of gases

Temperature fluctuations

Hands- sticks, marshmallows

Legs- *blanket*, lawn chairs, sharing night light

Shrugs shroud, eyes conceal, lips are sealed

Inhale, exhale

Paranoid, anxiety

Not raining, safe environment

Having fun in the backyard on a Sunday Night

Puff – Mist – Billow – Blanket – Swarm – Thunderhead – Nebulous – Cumulous

WRITE A POEM ABOUT

Dreams

"I dream what I Paint, and I paint my dream" – Vincent Van Gogh

I have a journal

When I wake up, pick it up

Try to describe the *mental picture* I was getting during my slumber

Tell the story, scribe the *image*

Astral projection

Into the atmosphere

Out of this world

In space, beyond our solar system

Exiting the galaxy

2001: A Space Odyssey

Rainbow's colors speed to plaid

So far away from home

Land of confusion, state of *trance*

Ball of light, entity *illusion*

Answers to all my questions

The reason for life and the universe

In bed, I asked for this to happen

Intention driven before sleep

Subconscious *vision*

Fancy a trip

Not a *fantasy*

Out of body

Souls truly exist

The physical is but a vessel

Supernatural experience

Awaken to a *thought* of purpose

In reality, write about it

In my dream

Fantasy – Trance – Thought – Image – Illusion - Mental Picture – Fancy – Vision

WRITE A POEM ABOUT

Food

Eat to live

I hate food

I hate the smell, I hate the look, I hate the *taste*

Loads of people love to discuss the topic

Ingredients, recipes, organic nutrients

I would eat paste if it gave me proper life sustenance

Calories, fat

You can't *digest* gum

I was told that it stays in your digestive system for 7 years

For 17 years I worked in a restaurant

Watch a massive man *masticate* pancakes

Watch an elderly woman thumpingly *chew* sirloin

Watch your stomach turn over, when an overweight person orders
an apple turnover, after eating an appetizer and an entrée

Serve several salads, then attempt adding it to your *diet*

Develop an eating disorder taking too many orders

Family friendly first offer hors d'oeuvres

Engrossing in too many odors

Bribe to *imbibe* alcohol

The apartment down the hall is cooking alien *cuisine*

The building reeks, impeding my nostrils

There is nowhere else to go

There is nothing else to do

Up and down the road

An entire room of your home dedicated to food

I eat the same thing over and over

Avoiding choice paralysis

Health is important, eat to live

A homeless man enjoys delicatessens thrown in a garbage, alongside rats

Gardens formed out of vacant lots

Cockroaches bombed multiple times

Bug sprayed fruit pesticides

Cherry flavored cough medicine

Edible panties and CBD gummies

When does food stop and paste begin

When will a pill replace my dinner

Wash your hands before eating, before leaving the bathroom

Eating issues, poisoned food killing us softly, slowly

Cancer, diabetes, cholesterol heart attacks

Break the body, medicate to fix, repeat the cycle

They own both sides of the coin

Food is just another political tool used to oppress the people

Start a garden in your backyard

Milk a cow, give scraps to chickens, recycle plastics

Battery power the electrons in the atmosphere

Harness electricity, minimize individual carbon footprint

Seeds are the highest currency of the desolate land

In the world of the blind, the one-eyed man is king

I will continue to eat to live

But I will never let food do the living for me

WRITE A POEM ABOUT

Carpe Diem

It's a game, it's fun

To *live* each day to the fullest

Play in every second, 86,400

No joy from the bullshit of Hedonism

Flesh pleasures, instant gratification

Jiminy cricket, the conscience

Tethered to the *nerve* like a rainbow bridge

Dare to let the Savior in

Nothing feels more real

Community contributions, group energy

Spiritual healing, forgiveness

Seize the opportunity to be a part of something beyond belief

Jesus is all-inclusive

No one should be poor, no one should be sick

The Lord makes us rich

Go forward with *boldness*

Dissolve all myths and illusions

I got my swagger by being humble

He provides confidence

To face any *endeavor* bravely

I am here for a reason

To show the strength of my God, his awesomeness

Beat the demons that try to creep into my thinking

Pluck out the impure

Use this body, brain, machine

Shine a light on His power, His goodness

Exist to express myself

We are not our past all added up

We are the sum of our future intentions

Without arrogance, show the world you're amazing

Have the *audacity* to give away the credit

Construct a philosophy to give and live without limits

I don't waste any seconds since

I learned with Him

All things are possible

Live – Pluck – Seize – Dare – Boldness – Endeavor - Audacity – Nerve

WRITE A POEM ABOUT

A Glance

Super quick

Took a *brief* look, what could it hurt

A fast glance

A photo *flash*

Gone in 60 seconds

Make an *impression*

Christian, atheist, new world religion

Manipulated versus independent decisions

Insecure, *shy*, impatient

I avoid *eye contact*

Sneak a *peek* over

Stare at lids and brows

Lying is easy to spot

A *fleeting* response

Eyes flicker from corner to corner

Blink once or twice before answering

The truth discovered

Deny the obvious; our minds create our reality

Gray matter mashed at the top

Skills mastered over a lifetime

Our time is up

Brief – Impression – Fleeting – Shy – Blink - Eye contact – Peek – Flash

WRITE A POEM ABOUT

Gratitude

Thank you, humbly

Every day is a gift

The present a present, my presence on Earth, His presence in me

A fresh start, renewed essence

September 21st; world gratitude day

We are all blessed, the sun is shining

Thank you, Bob Marley, may he rest in glory

Praise oxygen

Appreciate my nose for being able to filter air

Thankful for the hot and the cold

If you don't like Chicago weather, just wait 5 minutes it will change

We shed *grace*, show grace, display grace

Serenity is patience for an unsolvable situation

Courage is fighting for freedom

Wisdom is accepting we don't know the difference between right
and wrong

Jesus provided the blueprint

Problems abound but forgiveness *profound*

I pray for the *recognition*

Not to get overwhelmed in one's own self

Relive the experience of *humility*

Forgive the *debt*

Remember the abyss of depth

Torture, crucifixion, death, resurrection

It's an *honor* to pay tribute

It feels right to give thanks and praise

I eat communion to seal the covenant

I am so grateful Jesus died for my sins

I am so very grateful I know

I am on the path to Heaven

WRITE A POEM ABOUT

Paradise

2 tickets to paradise please

It could be so nice, if we took a holiday

To where the grass is green and the girls are pretty

I need to see *Eden*

The garden, Grandma take me home

Escort us to *nirvana*

Away from pain

A being in *Elysium*

Just like *heaven*

The cure for lame shame

I am a mortal creature guilty of sin

Immortality is a fallacy

Transport us above the innocuous

Bags packed we're ready to go

Take a drift to *bliss*

Delight in the abundance of love

We can't fathom a *utopia*

Once I'm done, no longer having fun

Get me out of this place

Eden – Elysium – Heaven – Bliss – Delight – Utopia – Transport – Nirvana

WRITE A POEM ABOUT

Marriage

Every day I am so happy

I am so in *love*

Thank God

Thank you, Hannah

For this *wedlock*

Holy *matrimony*

For this company, I am locked in

To your moods, your speeds, your needs

I am in complete awe of you

Every day, the way you exhibit kindness

Articulate your desires, *pledge* friendship

Secure our *alliance*, balance the checkbook

Insure our future

I appreciate you and I mean to mention it, every day

Remember to value the memories

Before and after the wedding

During *courtship*, a *couple* of dorks

It only took a few dates to know

In our souls, a *mate* to check the forever box

Laughter, romance, passion, counsel, ethics, morals

Goals, a family

We become one, twice

Anniversaries every 6 months

11/29 and 5/29

Renew our vows, true to our vows

Daily devotion, commitment eternal

WRITE A POEM ABOUT

A Choice

Every statement is an argument

In defense of or in compromise to

Are we in agreement

No one should be left alone

Every belief is a lie we choose

Emotionally driven

Passion vs. logic

A *marriage* of opposites

Built for empathy- easily manipulated

The plaintiff, the defendant

The *alternative*: hold the gavel

Charisma wins the *ballot*

Don't *challenge* authority

Color outside the lines

Shunned against the fence

Off the *path*, harassed

The moral *dilemma*, trolly problem

Seems you need to cheat to succeed

Immortality or the rapture

Being smart was not *popular*

Dorks and nerds were treated absurd

None of us believed they could achieve the dream

Now the king of the prom is a joke, broke with no job

Choices that hurt then hurt more older

Freedom, America John Wayne-Gacy was a clown

Police hunt you down

The phone is on listening to our conversations

Democracy means electing Puppet A or Puppet B

Coke or Pepsi, McDonald's or KFC

In the end, what is our destiny?

Will we destroy ourselves?

We only die because we accept it as an inevitability

Marriage – Path – Challenge – Alternative – Dilemma - Passion vs logic –
Popular – Ballot

WRITE A POEM ABOUT

Affection

Your audience awaits

Feel the grace

The *warmth* of our embrace

I promise I will show you affection

But not too much that it may *crush* your independence

I promise you have my *devotion*

By always being there *caring* with proper emotion

I am your dad forever

The thought alone makes my heart *tingle*

I promise I will treat your heart *tender*

You are a miracle

How I love your mother, that's *amore*

How I love you is unconditionally

No matter what

More than a moral, legal obligation

A gift, my wish, my baby

I promise I will never stop loving you

9 months as patient patients

Waiting to be a parent

A 43-year-old *itch* finally scratched

A dream fulfilled

I promise to never take it for granted

You are a miracle to be cherished

WRITE A POEM ABOUT

Confidence

There is nothing to fear but fear itself

High *morale*, don't be scared

Worried about your looks makes you look insecure

Look your best but don't let it handicap your moves

Paralyzed, quitters never win

Winners never quit

Wobbly knees, jaw to the floor

Low *esteem*, low self

Perpetual disappointment

Non-confrontational

Without integrity, you won't feel any *dignity*

Build one step at a time

Consistency is the key

Repetition is the mother of all skill

Learn abilities, gather *assurance* automatically

Trust the universe works

A code to *toughness*

Poise fake it till you make it

Tenacity to persevere

There is a choice in every moment

To go forward with *conviction*

Or choose to lose and not use the power the universe is offering

Tune into the frequency of belief

Confidence is a state of being

WRITE A POEM ABOUT

Expectations

Pulling back the barricade

Uncovered too many issues to be too specific

Felt like crying, here's a tissue wimp

Insults bullied into my identity

Obliterating the idea of unlimited *potential*

No *hope* for the future, a bad *notion*

Supposition- Murphy's Law

Design sabotage, I *promise* pain

Scout victims to feel my wrath

In a company that loves misery

Fall down pull everyone

Prospects, affiliates, partners

Dark *motive* to hurt

Discovered development change

Think life into being

We get what we expect

Thoughts lead to words, lead to actions

One small push moves mountain

The lesson- intend good to great expectations

You'll get what you think either way

Promise – Notion – Supposition – Design – Motive – Prospects – Hope – Potential

WRITE A POEM ABOUT

Home

I will buy a *house*

A dream fulfilled

To own my own home

Build from bottom to top

Tenement to pent

Trap to mansion

An *apartment* with heart

A brazier for burning coal

Hearth fireside a wall

Painting a window, vision a clearer mirror

Chopping down a mountain with the edge of my hand

Welcomed back with open arms

Forgiveness, patience, love

A place to stay and move away from

Creating a new

Empty nest, unlimited possibilities

Filling the *kitchen* with appliances

Filling the halls with laughter

Filling the bedroom with passion

Adding security to the surroundings

Photos displaying memories

There's more to a home than a mortgage

More to a *cottage* than carpet and couches

To raise a family, it takes a *village*

It's the sniff, sound, tongue, feel, view

I will buy a house

Fix the roof if needed

Replace the broken windows

But more than real estate

My real dream

A home so full of love, so wholesome

Hosting great grandchildren for every holiday celebration

House – Fireside – Village – Kitchen – Hearth – Cottage – Apartment – Tenement

WRITE A POEM ABOUT

Independence

I love myself

I am free

The shackles of 9 to 5, 8 to 430

The pursuit to happiness

I embrace the journey

Force of will build *strength*

The *autonomy* of my morning routine

Exercise, affirmations, actualize *assuredness*

Accomplishment *confidence*

Self-reliance, discipline

Overcoming toxic programming

Rewiring thought patterns

Sovereign in mind

Inner *determination*

Training to enhance the new paths

Repetition is the mother of all skill

Time is the only limit to learning

Fear for survival

Trapeze rope, back flips, balance in the air, levitate without wings

Dreams fulfilled, true independence

Ultimate *freedom*

I am a millionaire, I am successful

The buddha monk without a want

Serving my soul's purpose

Amazing beauty seen by the beholder

Letting go to move forward

Freedom – Sovereign - Self-reliance – Autonomy – Strength – Confidence –
Assuredness – Determination

WRITE A POEM ABOUT

Laughter

Burst onto the scene mean green

Living the dream, for the big screen, big things

Achieve, believe, self-esteem

Positive mindset; His word

The *merriment - medicine*

Fresh fruit for the *belly*

A wolf *howl* at the moon

Hallelujah *rejoice* in the sun

I got that inner smile

Ears open, message heard, message relayed

Play with the toy boy *joy* cry

Koy annoy shrewd *shriek* corny

His name we are allowed to speak Jesus

I didn't start very religious

Glory image abundance wellness

Path to happiness, path to an easier life

Pray morning, day, afternoon, evening and at goodnight

Spark the insight to write, recite

Edit, re-write, and re-recite

Post, boast, coast, toast, share

Make the most of my talents and abilities

Laugh at any obstacle in front of me

Like I don't care

Bash the past insecurity into obscurity

Confidence to make it amazing, wherever I go

The strength to stand in front of a giant

With only a sling and a stone

WRITE A POEM ABOUT

Passion

The cleverer teacher/preacher is cool

But what really, truly moves people?

Emotion, bless the message with *zest*

On fire *desire,* on display every day

In the *heat* of the moment

Cool, calm, collected

Present an argument

Logic dictates the answer

Persuasively persist with *ardor*

Layered *intensity*

Can you handle the truth?

Clarity, peace resolute

Compassion, a *fervor* for empathy

Lust for salvation

Appeal to the *zeal* to seal the covenant

Jesus what would you do?

A Christ's type passion for life

Scribe design divine prodigy

The passion within me

His plan, our future

Together, we flow down the river

Uncover/discover it's up to my action

Unleash God's power

He is in control

I breathe the fire the world turns

Ardor – Fervor – Intensity – Heat – Zest – Lust – Desire – Zeal

WRITE A POEM ABOUT

Moving On

I am moving on from trauma

Not a victim any longer, stronger

I praise the pain

Everyone makes mistakes

I have lies for which I am ashamed

Complained, inflicted self-blame

Negative statements *hasten* the negative trajectory

I was destined for depression

Childhood problems don't impact me now

I overcame

Writing my story, therapeutic

I *continue* to *push* through it

Go forth forgiving

Slow process, slow *progress*

Disciplined patience, as long as it takes

To reach to a new destination

Happiness, contentment, fulfillment

Launch out of bed with conviction

The *momentum* makes it faster and easier

Amazing, awesome, affirmations, again a process

Reprogramming my brain

Retraining my muscles

Automatic habits, *proceed* with caution

Question all my beliefs

Found answers dynamic and tragic

Morals, ethics, philosophy

My new motto: be in tune

The future is a series of probabilities depending on the choices we make now

I am moving on

Aware of where I came from

WRITE A POEM ABOUT

Bliss

Instant gratification

Euphoria in the moment

The girl next door, born and raised in Compton

Pour some sugar on me

What I got, sublime

Living in *paradise* city

Current state of *nirvana*, illin' nois'

Come as you are, my boy

Bundle of *joy*

All *glory* to the angels that brought you down from Heaven

The *rapture* will bring us back up

It ain't hard to tell, human nature

This must be the place of *completeness*

Audio, visual, sensory input check

Learning with every breathe you take

Wrapped in kisses and Huggies underneath a swaddle

Lose yourself in the music

Memory, us alone in the midday light

Feeling *ecstasy,* kid cuddling

Hope I live to tell the secrets I have learned

No doubts, shake it off

Jesus walks on water and so can I

After it freezes, breastmilk stores 6 months

Time is on our side

Joy – Euphoria – Paradise – Rapture – Glory – Nirvana – Ecstasy – Completeness

WRITE A POEM ABOUT

Wonder

The wonderful wizard of here

Exert, conserve, go fast, go slow, human nature

Survival of the fittest

One day at a time, follow the yellow lines on the highway

Listen to the GPS, look it up

Immediate gratification

Everyone's watching porn

Admiration to a figment of imagination

A brain transformed

Generational behavior

X, Z, Millennials

Forget the *reverence* of elders

Wisdom washed down the sewage drain

Grandma has become delusional, Alzheimer's

Baby booms to start the day

I *marvel* at his learning

Object *fascination*, toys, anything he can reach goes in his mouth

Feed the *curiosity*

We eat political rhetoric

Media manipulated missions, the signs of the times

My meditation quiet moment

Weed out the *perplexity* of reality

Whistle while you work around chaos

Overcoming objections, negotiating internationally

Life is like all the chocolates in the box

A mystery to be in *awe* of

Art becomes science, theory into law

Particles of stars perfect you

Electric *jolt* to the heart, a defibrillator

Sometimes we could all use an extra push

Awe – Marvel – Curiosity – Jolt – Reverence – Admiration – Perplexity – Fascination

WRITE A POEM ABOUT

Forgiveness

I don't deserve forgiveness

I did some stuff that was horrendous

Unforgivable

I will always remember the sin

I attempted to *repent* but relapsed once again

Robbed *charity*

Humiliated family

Let anger win, lost self-control

Emotional intelligence practices out the door

I don't expect *lenience* at my *absolution*

Mercy for the weak

Torture to the strong that hurt

No *grace* for demons

Against *compassion* for liars, thieves, and cheaters

Life for the guilty convicted

Find *clemency* only in the cave of wonders

3 wishes won't grant freedom

For the man who sold the world

And for those who have sold their souls

Clemency – Compassion – Mercy – Absolution – Lenience – Charity – Grace – Repent

WRITE A POEM ABOUT

Imagination

Vivid dreams lucid

I scribble words to describe the images

Make a story, create a movie

Van Gogh art

The *fantastic invention*

Rapidly advancing technology

Images displayed 3rd and 4th dimensionally

Holographically *stimulating* senses

Neural manipulation

Pinocchio punishes himself with drugs and alcohol

Calling for sex from the comfort of an anonymous cellphone

Mickey murders

Masterful *artistry*

The star treks a new *enterprise*

Wreck em Ralph or Wrexham

Millionaire investments

Trending Reddit comments

Take my simple skill to billions

Originality is worth enough to quit my jobs

Behind the scenes, religion and politics are the best topics to not talk about

Flip the script

A *vision* of eliminating a worthless existence

Hustling towards goals

Imagine a balance in my life

Writing, acting, producing, directing

Family, friends, work, relaxation

Getting paid to be creative

Getting paid very well in fact

Rock the bells, salute the sample

We are the world, we are the champions

Wake up affirmations, motivational speeches

I am living the dream

Vivid – Invention – Fantastic – Stimulating – Vision -Enterprise – Originality – Artistry

WRITE A POEM ABOUT

Peace

Peace was easy

Stop fighting

Then I realized, I'm not living

Anything good is worth fighting for

I kept giving up

No *joy* came from my *tranquility*

The *amity* soon became anxiousness

Confidence reduced to squalor

Skipping the competition

Crawling under the hurdle

Avoiding confrontation

Can't have *harmony* all alone

Missing *unity*, missing community

Lost friends don't come back

No *truce* for the grudge

In *order* to reduce the friction

Pretend it's all love

Peace is *quiet*

I'd rather be loud

I learned to speak my opinion

Even if that means war

Order – Truce – Unity – Amity – Quiet – Harmony – Tranquility – Joy

WRITE A POEM ABOUT

Love

Valentine's rhyme line

Bind mind mine yours

Yearning, turning, churning, learning

Time heals, time flies, time flows

Time is on my side, in time the truth is told

I think it is time for this old shlub

Wubba lubba dub dub

In the club hugs, mean mugs, shoulder shrugs

Barter harder for your *ardor*

Wocka flocka fliggity *flame*

Connection *affection* fifty frames four seconds

Locomotion *emotion* roller coaster

Fake *fondness* fortune 500 philanthropist

Left for dead without love

The *rapture* ripped the ripe right out, the righteous ones

Idol *adoration* complication

Adoring ego driven cringing wisdom

Searching, lurching, churching

Words weak, actions louder

Prouder, powder shrouder coward, no longer

Thanks for all the blessings

Lessons, check-ins, bredren

To all my enemies, I forgive

I got nothing but love for ya

Adoration – Affection – Yearning – Flame – Emotion – Ardor – Fondness –
Rapture

WRITE A POEM ABOUT

Romance

I have more romance to give

Please tell me you also love me

I want to hear it

I want to feel it, residual encouragement

Meet, *flirtation*, sex, *amour*, marriage

Then kids, till death, or divorce

Souls mesh, lives *entangle*

Vulnerabilities become a force

Imperfections are the perfections

Family is sacred, no *intimacy* from a stranger

Individual memories, social legacy, historical accuracy

Don't misinterpret my *passion*

My wife has my *desire*

Blaze the heart, light her fire

The *thrill* of our *affair*

Inside jokes we share

A darling treading its first water

The palmate erratic

The effort we put into our relationship

Under the surface; on the surface

Our dates were not sporadic

Special surprises planned every weekend

Every day nurturing texts

Future figurations

Husband, wife, mom, dad

Today the son's reflection mirrors our inner selves

Congruent contentment between us

It's all been worth it

My happy wife, my happy life

I do it all for the love

Thrill – Amour – Affair – Flirtation – Entangle – Intimacy – Passion – Desire

WRITE A POEM ABOUT

A Secret

A group of 2

One always lies the other always tells the truth

Intelligence is knowing how to choose

Unlock the *cryptic* message

Desperate thoughts lead to desperate measures

Hidden desires *clouded* the responsibility

Arm cuts, mirror punch

Maturity is doing the right thing

Keeping secrets is dangerous

Lying will flush the trust out of a relationship

Being honest can be worse

Hush to the outside world

Thoughts lead to words, leads to sadness

In some instances, keep things *private*

That's none of their concern

A shadow of doubt

The mystery of faith

Flames of passion lit the *dark* room

Eyes crossed in the *mist* of candle vapors

Warm body, cold air

Instant *regret* afterward

Buried beneath the surface

Groveling for forgiveness

I will just have to live with it

A magician never reveals his secret

The shame game; there is no one else to blame

Why risk it

WRITE A POEM ABOUT

Solitude

No sharing

No tweets on X

No airing dirty laundry

Nothing too intimate, nothing too personal

Trolls lies told, grab all the gold

TikTok holds no lore

No lure to fish for YouTube fandom

Stay *alone*, avoiding hypocritical rationalizations

Seclusion from all social media platforms

Off-grid in the *remote* wilderness

Attempts at *isolation* are futile

The *introvert* never heard any applause

The *recluse* never saw the raw beauty in the abilities of Michael
Jordan or Wayne Gretzky

We miss 100% of the shots we don't take

I pray the hospital doesn't microchip my baby

Private thoughts exposed Kanye West

Chemtrail the trailer park

Fluoride in the water

Solo cups all over the place

A *hermit* crab pack of lion pride alpha males

Snakes in the grass, actor activists

Woke Karens, handy Andy's mansplaining

Join the discord

Podcast your thoughts

NFT the memes

Conspiracy theory broadcast news

Hilarious jokes suppressed claim oppressed

Rude solitude, confinement

Dissidence the sentence unreasonable, no rehabilitation

Never given a second chance

All of us cancelled

Alone – Isolation – Seclusion – Recluse – Introvert – Private – Remote –
Hermit

WRITE A POEM ABOUT

Music

One good thing, when it hits you, you feel no pain

Name that *tune* in any season Gershwin

An influential *instrumental* by DJ Scottie Phresh

Check out my *melody*

I like what I like, not what's *popular*

Conductor of an uncoordinated *orchestra*

Ska song battle between horns and saxophones

Polka accordion according to the king

Arithmetic in the *rhythm*

The *choral* connection of birds with cars

Dance to the beat of your heart

Feeling good is the point

A *hymn* for him or her, the radio has the answer

The devil is in rock'n'roll

The preacher prefers the Gospel

My baby does the hacky-panky

Artists go broke, the label keeps the money

Royalties are stolen from protagonist punks

Request the sample or get sued

Rebelling against a corrupt, vicious system

The news, views, politics, religion

The truth is in the music, anyone can listen

Ignore the irrelevant, silence can be the best sound

Wearing noise dampening headphones while riding the subway

Lost and found in nature, in spirit, in your own head

Lost in the ecstasy of the moment, listening to music

International, country, edm

Hip-hop is not dead

I used to love her and I still do

One good thing that we can all rely on

When it hits you, you feel no pain

Melody – Hymn – Instrumental – Orchestra – Popular – Tune – Choral –
Rhythm

WRITE A POEM ABOUT

Nighttime

Awakened by screaming. Our son came running into our bedroom crying, "Mommy, Daddy, I had a scary dream." "That's alright buddy," I said, then I let him jump into our bed. Immediately, he started snoozing; my wife was snoring; it was a *moonless* night, curious the drapes were open. Laying there seemed like forever, I became *sleepless*. Insomnia got me hungry. To the fridge, tripped over the *black* cat in the *darkness* of the voyeur. Opened the fridge, no light, chugged a bottle of water but had to spit it out, it was a bottle of breastmilk. I guess the lights were too *dim*, in the kitchen. I flicked the switch, but nothing happened. Eerie, plus the numbers on the microwave clock were rotating. I thought nothing of it, avoiding the *shadow* creeping up behind me, I ran back to the room. Attempted to slide in through the side of the bed, but there was no room. Pulled over the covers, *vigil*, to discover my child had been cloned. 2 sons' wide-awake jumping up and down on the bed. I fell over in shock. One son fell over and rolled off the edge of the bed. But before he hit the ground, 2 more took his place instead. Now, 3 kids are jumping on the bed. My wife is still sleeping while they are bouncing off and on her head. As one falls off the bed, two more jump back on. The cycle keeps repeating. The kids are all jumping up and down, bouncing, laughing, and giggling. Multiplying boys rapidly, then I start laughing, getting really giddy too. I realize it's my dream. My son wasn't having a scary dream. The nighttime nightmare is mine to endure. I have the power. I laugh again, open my eyes, take a breath to recover. Get up out of bed, and there is no kid, my son is in his crib, as I left him. My one innocent, precious baby boy. I can't go back to sleep now, I'm *wakeful*, grateful for every moment. That nighttime nightmare was awesome. Go ahead and prepare my cereal with real milk. And before I forget, write it all down in my dreams journal.

WRITE A POEM ABOUT

A Sunny Day

Today is a beautiful day

You are a beautiful person

A hot day

The sun is *shining*

I hope you stay hydrated

I love you

I'm always concerned for your well-being

Please use sunscreen

Claritin *clarion* allergies

You look *radiant* in your bathing suit

I *bask* in your wet form

Walking barefoot through the flowers

Your body seems to glow

Running on the grass

Playing bags/cornhole

Grilled hamburgers, hot dogs, beer

Describing my job to in-laws

Making the scene feel *summery*

A July 4th summary

In the evening, fireworks were *brilliant*

The black sky became *luminous*

The sun blasting all day helps you appreciate the cool end

I'm still in a *haze*

From all the eating and swimming

Family and friends

A celebration of life

Honoring the beauty of a sunny day

Luminous – Summery – Shining – Clarion – Radiant – Brilliant – Bask – Haze

WRITE A POEM ABOUT

Change

Dear Mr. President,

Equality seems heaven-sent

We petition, protest, then riot

Still, I see no changes

The Bill of Rights needs *revision*

Inclusion instead of systematic racism

Infer a *season* of *variance* instead of incurring years of oppression

Instilling obedience, installing tracked microchips into citizen's
wrists

In the future, there will be a *metamorphosis*

A *transmutation* of ideals

I just want to be there to witness the *transition*

Describe the paradigm *shift*

Real-life movies

How history is told, stories passed down to young from old

Control the perspective, *switch* who you hear

They manipulate the media, push a devilish agenda

Diminish our freedoms

The only thing we should fear is fear itself

But we are so scared of change

Let the box think for us

The couch is too comfortable

Shift – Transition – Metamorphosis – Revision – Season – Switch –
Transmutation – Variance

WRITE A POEM ABOUT

Jealousy

Hey, what do you want

I got it

The *covetous* status of my brother

His bank account, his respect

I got that hot chick, she works for me

I am a pimp

I've bested the competition

In this game of life

You wish you could change the past

Go back in time

To fix the fact you lacked any discipline

Get rich quick instead of putting in effort

Agonize over what could have been

Antagonism for your best friend

I am mad at you; you didn't have it as bad as me

The *rivalry* was one-sided

Overwhelming trauma

Motivation beaten in

You never listened, you did the opposite out of *spite*

Envy of mediocrity

Hold a *grudge* then cringe at their success

Animosity against a thousand-naire

On my way to a millionaire lifestyle, net worth multi

The only *strife* we could have both had this life

Why were we jealous of each other brother?

Rivalry – Envy – Antagonism – Animosity – Spite – Grudge – Covetous –
Strife

WRITE A POEM ABOUT

Pride

Unattached, ashamed, depressed

The mind playing tricks on me

Replaying the moment over and over

Groundhog Day, wasted years

Learn, think and grow rich

Get over it, no pity

Ostentation, fake it till you make it

You only live once

Pump up the *ego*, the *pomp*

The *lion* in the jungle doesn't stop to smell the roses

He attacks the gazelle

Boast in the appropriate moments

Show *confidence* accomplish one new thing every day

Take the path laid out before you

Follow the yellow brick road

Create *dignity* by honoring your word

Too cool to read, to go to the library

It's free to study

Arrogance blocks most people

Be humble, don't ask for it to be easier, ask yourself to get better

Practice 10,000 hours

Nothing, no one's stopping you

Except foolish pride

Lion – Dignity – Pomp – Ostentation – Arrogance – Boast – Confidence –
Ego

WRITE A POEM ABOUT

A Surprise

No metaphors, no play on words

Intently seeking honesty, comfort

Vomit flavored jelly beans all of the *sudden*

When I saw Him grab her arm

Grief is extremely tough

Epiphany, no longer a hand to hold

A surprise, I am alive, not in jail

She kept me free

Godsend- Godson in my ears for years

Exclaim hallelujah at Boppa's church

All the lessons learned

They held me and gave me everything I ever needed

My wife, my son, my purpose

Tragedy averted, dealt with, handled, circumvented

A rainbow after the storm

Seriously, my mom passed, my stepdad passed

We had a miscarriage, now we are having a baby boy

My family is my miracle

It does *baffle* me

I can feel *astound* joy

Emotional process, collateral beauty

Unexpected understanding

An intimate relationship with Him

I was surprised by how much

Love can *ambush*

At a sad time

WRITE A POEM ABOUT

Scared

From the depths of my soul

Always had a reason to be

Trauma at home

In true reflection I can begin to see

Where I was scared, and why

The peak point should be above me but I always thought it was behind

I had a high, now I'm older, lower somehow

Not financially further farther along

A Father and Husband *unsure* how to it's all going along

Sometimes I fear my wife hates me, or my son won't love me

Irrational *panic* sets in that I'm worthless again

I begin to spin, *afraid* in every situation

My life is in *danger*, paranoia

I am my own worst enemy

I hurt myself to assert myself

Putting pepper sauce on my bump to stop biting

Aghast it doesn't help

Checking my ego at the door

At *risk* of losing it all

Do I take life seriously

How far do I have to fall to hit rock bottom

Confidence broken down to pieces, no hard consonants

Softly sounded, a voice unheard

Weak sauce actions, my desperation

The chili needed better ingredients

Not fancy doctorate, proof by example

Cannot be *fearful* of the explanation

One mind, one life

Responsibility dictates my terms

Previous outbursts *stricken* from the record

My heart is pure

Aghast – Stricken – Fearful – Danger – Risk – Unsure – Panic – Afraid

WRITE A POEM ABOUT

The Night Sky

Airplanes in the night sky do not look like shooting *stars*

Twinkling wishes flickering in the distance

Fading falling dying suns

As a kid I was scared of the dark

My night lights were black lit *constellations*

Glowing stickers on the ceiling

After a month, the *glimmer* gave me headaches

I quit wishing

American dream, nightmare Freddy

Get up, go to the job, go home, watch tv

Insanity, insomnia

Go to school, work at night, 30 days of hustling

60 years of muscling, no rest for the wicked

Destined bleakness, the vast *blackness*

Work my shift, then I'm wired, *wakeful*

Imagine taking sleeping pills having cut-off eyelids or forced open
ones like in A Clockwork Orange

Vampire consuming social media

Waste the day, waste time, waste of life

Daylight, moonlight, midnight

Watch the world turn

Wish the twist was faster, the *pitch* wasn't off centered

Hoping the view from Heaven is better

Debating the weather or whether or not to whether the storm

Predicting the outcome, gambling the score

Contemplating wants, hopes, needs

In the clear night sky, I can see the future

The sun will come out tomorrow

Stars – Blackness – Moonlight – Midnight – Pitch – Constellations –
Glimmer – Wakeful

WRITE A POEM ABOUT

Tragedy

Overcame *adversity*, no longer depressed

Without pills or medicine

Only meditation and exercise

I earned self-respect

Awake, alive, and thriving

Sleep is the cousin to *death*

Arrange the new day, follow the light

Set goals, follow the steps

Fought the *doom* of gloom

Broke the so-called family *curse*

Generational physical, sexual, emotional, verbal, and also,
substance abuse

Affliction cured through disciplined hard work

No addiction can stir my morning peace

Averted *catastrophe* by taking responsibility

Everybody has a tragedy

Everyone has a trauma

I am survivor, not a victim

Triumphant spirit

Harder, stronger because of it

Turned my story into glory

Misfortune into fortune

Emotional pain into financial gain

Rape into rap

Molestation into manifestation

Multiple malicious memories given to me by my uncle when I was
8 years old

I could have let that effect, defect, the rest of my life

I did let it *wreck* many years, when I kept it a secret

Go home or go bold

To overcome has begun a new life

Now I have a wife, and a son on the way

Used it all the tragedy to make me who I am today

Scottie Awesome Powers

Doom – Adversity – Death – Wreck – Catastrophe – Affliction – Misfortune –
Curse

WRITE A POEM ABOUT

A Pet

Pinnacle is my *dog*

Apples is my *cat*

I got the pup, Pinnie, from the Wolfpack Shelter

When my mom passed, we inherited the Maine Coon; Apples

Can you believe that he is 23 years old

My min-pin boy just turned 4

My stepdad had a *snake* named Bubba

He used that as his email handle for A.O.L. for many years

My brother had tons of Teenage Mutant Ninja *Turtle* t-shirts and
toys growing up

I didn't play with toys; I played shoot the *rabbit* at duck hunt

A pet is a big responsibility

We could all use a good *companion* to keep us *company*

Don't make your pets do weird stuff

Like join pageants or wear clothing

Make a *parrot* say bad words

Treat your pets good

Give them treats when their good

They will treat you well back

With universally understood

Unconditional love

Companion – Dog – Cat – Turtle – Rabbit – Snake – Company – Parrot

WRITE A POEM ABOUT

Chance

Totally *random;* the page opens

The urge yearning

Release fury while a furry feline tries to steal my attention

A *gamble*, my patience is limited

Focus is a learned skill

Is it *luck*, or is it *destiny*

Fake *fortune* dreams

Roulette at the casino

Every desperate idea tested

Project *providence*

Thought, intent, assume, attract

The publisher funds a material-gaining lifestyle

The writer goes *remote* to find inspirational material

Fate is going back and analyzing

The road that got me here didn't appear itself

No helicopter propellers

No one master's a craft by chance

10,000 hours

For me, it has been more like 100,000

WRITE A POEM ABOUT

Forgetting

Welcome to the brain cell graveyard where alcohol and marijuana
are responsible for memory losses

Good times sometimes *omit* the details

No one needs to know

Drunk in jail

We lie to ourselves

Give up, cry

Consign to not try

Wish to go back in time

Have a *clean slate*

Failures erased

We *scorn* the path of our fate

Neural pathways are more ingrained as we age

It becomes more difficult to *disremember* the hurt

Easier to feel comfortable

Less struggle, fall in line with the crowd

Accept neglect

Beat down become powerless

We can change

Gain strength forget the irrelevant

Escape the tragedy

Obliterate it into *oblivion*

All those triggers hinder our evolution

Puff, puff, *pass* the stress to a best friend

Better yet a therapist

Do whatever it takes to get over it

Remember the memories more pleasing

I love you; I love myself, I love everyone

Forget to hate become like Lucy Whitmore

50 first dates, daily amnesia

Oblivion – Disremember – Consign – Escape – Pass – Omit – Scorn – Clean slate

WRITE A POEM ABOUT

Virtue

No *merit* for a state's attorney

Truth, justice

The American way is wrong

Imperial un-*ethical* judges

Non-*righteous* diplomate hypocrites

Rule with impunity, declaring im-*purity*

Stealing *charity* from those they deem un-*worthy*

The non-*paragon* with a gown and gavel

Uptight in a fake *upright* chair

Uprooting communities, looting families

Sentencing more years later in the afternoon than earlier

Secret brotherhoods, the lawyers go first

An impeccable record for giving the maximum

I can't see the virtue in imprisoning without rehabilitating

The situation keeps getting worse

How do we fix a broken system

Only the rich get the benefits

God said the meek shall inherit the Earth

When?

99 percent of it, is ruled by the 1

Paragon – Merit – Ethical – Righteous – Purity – Charity – Worthy –
Upright

WRITE A POEM ABOUT

Conflict

I hate you

I love you

My brother, my enemy

My opponent, my teammate, my *rival*

The *fray* is petty

Fights, jealousy

Friction from repeated failure

To *embroil* for the thrill

Believing we are both the *protagonist* of the same story

Clash of titans

Strife for life

A *breach* of trust

Confused by illusions and myths

Lies embedded into our embroidery

Branding ourselves with children's sweat

Posting personal problems to the public

Contest criticism from loved ones

Rehab the relationship

My evil counterpart

The mirror's reflection

Fray – Breach – Clash – Rival – Contest – Embroil – Protagonist – Strife

WRITE A POEM ABOUT

Strength

Mohammed is a strong name

But bias based skin color baby

Unfortunately, perception is reality

Understand the Powers' *power*

Sexy look, strong *muscle*, intelligent quotient

Grow the *sinew*, grow the cerebrum

Standard grandpa patriarch

Watch the paint dry miss the *pith*

The path to here

Stunning stamina, *vitality*, grit

I envy the *potency* of sperm

Fully focused concentrated effort with a smile

Egg, crack, yoke, joke- no

My plate is served

A made bed to lie

Prepared room, stuff stocked, walls primed

Founded *fortitude*, family first

Flesh and blood around the eyes and in the chin

In that moment I knew

Time is on our side

If you've got your *health*, you've got everything

I reside, I will protect you with all my strength

Vitality – Fortitude – Health – Power – Muscle – Sinew – Pith – Potency

WRITE A POEM ABOUT

Insanity

Doing the same thing every and over again expecting different
results

That's not the true definition

It's just a myth like everything else

Columbus didn't discover America

The lies they tell kids

Create *mania* intently

Easy to control the *incoherent*

Hard to handle the organized

Propagate that sex is better than following religious tradition

Every emotion is a *neurosis* that needs to be medicated

Unjustified murder in the middle of the street

A state of *delirium* across the nation

Invent covid and enforce imprisonment

No more riots, no more protests

We see the *folly* but feel powerless

A *delusion* so embedded in our minds

Praying at night

That our favorite sports team will win

Television manipulation

Brainwashed slave to the system

Making excuses to be useless

Eating stupid amounts of food

The lunar *lunacy* astrology

Actually, seems more appealing as a viable explanation

The laws of nature

Bent by the law of attraction

An *irrational* comprehension

Of our artificial intelligence

*Delirium – Lunacy – Mania – Irrational – Incoherent – Delusion – Neurosis
– Folly*

WRITE A POEM ABOUT

Challenges

To *overcome* the pain of trauma

Odds are against you

Trials will be endured

Questions will not have answers

Explanations will defy reason

Dare to be great

Create *moxie*

Persevere it will get better

The *obstacle* was made to break thru

Battle the *gauntlet*

Ignore fear

Humans hear music

Birds hear humans

Beauty is perspective

Maintain the positive mindset

Get up, be free

On purpose, enjoy the journey

Take on challenges

Embrace the opportunity

Odds – Trials – Dare – Gauntlet – Moxie – Overcome – Persevere – Obstacle

WRITE A POEM ABOUT

A Fragrance

A flagrant fragrance

I hate her smell

The pussy reeks

Her breath stinks

The sweat isn't sweet

The vagina is too vinegary

I can't stand her touch

Body *balm* ashy

Calice heals, farmers tan

Big burps, giant farts

Her odor never produces a *savory aroma*

After a deuce, strong *musk*

Dirty underwear, stained drawers

Piles of laundry

Bouquet of disgust

Dirt protrudes fingernails

Dust-ball Pigpen

Intoxicate the senses

Sloppy, runny makeup

Honeysuckle dripped down a bull calf

Attract bees, flies cluster

Rotten food burrowing between braces

Taste poop

Huge ass droops

Can't be *subtle* against such gross physical attributes

A flagrant fragrance

Bouquet – Balm – Aroma – Savory – Musk – Honeysuckle – Intoxicate –
Subtle

WRITE A POEM ABOUT

Dilemma

Truly in a *bind*

How am I going to survive?

Pick a career, Roadhouse or Grit

I despise restaurants

Chicken no head

Too fast phone calls

Always be closing

50 customers in the cue waiting

Training a *mess*

Scrape by on pathetic checks

Excuse excess taxes

Quagmire, entrepreneur- never

Mouse in the maze

Impasse ablaze

Comfort or public

Alone, amongst strangers

Past stress, present stagnant

Sweatpants, no shower

Crumb catcher, uniform

Fork in the road

Cockroach, cardboard to go *boxed in*

Hard *choice* headset or burnt skin

Money, money, money

I won't know for sure until I calculate the wear and tear

Extra expenses, extra preparation

One heck of a decision

My child in the middle

My purpose, my why

The *plight* of a father

Willed to provide

Professional customer service

Bind – Choice - Boxed in – Impasse – Scrape – Plight – Mess – Quagmire

WRITE A POEM ABOUT

Faith

I believe in God almighty, maker of Heaven and Earth

I have faith in Jesus; His only son

He died on the cross, so I could have eternal life

He sacrificed himself for the covenant of all

Through Him I get to know the Father

To be human is to be a sinner

Certainty in the everlasting grants me *confidence*

Belief in a higher power, reassures my worth

The *dogma* compels my *conviction*

When I *trust* the Lord, I am forgiven

Fealty through the Holy Communion

The body and blood of Christ

Ceremonies and traditions passed down generations

Epigenetics of worship

I know I will see my parents again

The doctrine is studied to understand

No one is perfect

Adoration for miracles

They don't just happen you have to believe they will

Starting over takes one step

One set of footprints in the sand when you feel overwhelmed

Whenever you need help

Ask and you shall receive

A kingdom in paradise awaits all who believe

Adoration – Certainty – Trust – Fealty – Belief – Conviction – Confidence –
Dogma

WRITE A POEM ABOUT

Truth

Truth and opinions get mixed up

Managerial decisions, who to start

The team needs *genuine* talent

Fact stats not skewed

Graphs are easily manipulated

Heart is hard to measure

In *reality*, there is no *certainty*

Quantum particle probability

Alternate dimension, looney toons

Mandella effect, George with a tail, Berenstein Bears

Time travel Delorean, groundhog, dog ate my homework

Lies are in the eyes

Hide your *candor*

Roofie cocktail party, hidden rooms, flash the camera

Show your *authentic* self

Manipulated by subliminal messages

Primed brain against *honesty*

Tell a fake story to an imaginary friend

Corrupted *purity*, savage lessons

Insufficient information, ignorant idiots

Unclear message, miscommunication

Unexplainable metaphor, unnerving body language

Asked to hold back valuables

The black swan danced at her own funeral

Candor – Purity – Reality – Fact – Certainty – Genuine – Honesty –
Authentic

WRITE A POEM ABOUT

Inequality

I heard there are tunnels under L.A.

It lets the Hollywood elite escape traffic

Quick exits at the next studio or stadium

They even have gas stations and Starbucks

But the stars don't pay no bucks

Isolation out of touch

White *privilege* switched to rich privilege

Walls and gates to expand the *difference*

The *injustice* was built up around us

Judicial *bias* based on tiredness

Get a lighter sentence when the case is heard earlier in the day

Afford a good lawyer who dug up dirt on the State's attorney

Systematic *racism*, more opportunities in my resumé

All I know is, when I was arrested it could have been way worse

Disparity in the numbers

Percentage of blacks imprisoned

Imagine being chased, captured and then lynched

Especially because you knew how to do business

You took money out another man's pocket

Being educated gets you hunted

They keep their secrets from being discovered

The illuminati will never illuminate how to attain and maintain a fortune

School teaches obedience

Born under *misfortune*

Swear its *unfair* political activist

In the zeitgeist we are all zombies

– Disparity – Privilege – Misfortune

Unfair – Injustice – Racism – Difference – Bias – Disparity – Privilege – Misfortune

WRITE A POEM ABOUT

Maturity

Complicated topics require finesse

Adult discussions; politics, religion, sex

Career, marriage, kids

Wealth acquisition, on the job training

Real serious matters

Speech with *sophistication*

NLP practitioner certification

Master 10,000 hours

Taxes and tragedies

Maturity means emotional intelligence

Automatic habits, ingrained behaviors

Lazy creatures seek comfort

Prime my home for success

Running shoes next to the bed

Ask to be *apt*, not for it to be easier

Become *advanced* in the thing

Ride the wave of momentum

Life is but a dream

Row your boat, pick your stream

Grow *ripe* vegetables in the garden

Seeds, *experience*, memories

Give advice to those who seek it

Offer *wisdom* in a form that's creative

Driven by a sole purpose

My soul's purpose

Pass down my wisdom

Experience – Adult – Sophistication – Wisdom – Prime – Ripe – Advanced –
Apt

WRITE A POEM ABOUT

Loneliness

Pain, hurt, sadness, and loneliness

Can't wait to buy all that stuff up

Depression isn't real

It's a state of mind

Like Michael Jordan or Patrick Mahomes can get into the zone

In 2020 I got married

Broke the *monotony* of all that hardcore jazz

That had gotten to be a little out of control

Living on the edge, living on *empty*

Gas tank, bank account, refrigerator

I'm having illusions all these confusions driving me mad inside

My mind is playing tricks on me

Lil ghetto boy punching the concrete on Halloween

Seclusion can cause physical bruises to the brain and body

Non-inclusion simply for the amusement of the so-called elite

Security gates, armed guards are mercenaries

Apathetic lambs of *silence*

With open arms the wind beneath my wings

At a party; the Humpty Dance is your chance to do the hump

Mixing my thoughts with others' quotes

Confidence is not *quiet*

All roads lead back to home, West Virginia

Solitary confinement true torture

Misery loves company

Committing crimes to back inside Mr. Brooks

In *isolation*, how is anyone ever supposed to get better

The system/matrix simulation is flawed

Read books, watch videos, take courses

Longing for your touch brother

Sensitive in my own skin

I got over it, you can get over it

Analyze the issue, use a tissue

Stop making the same mistake

For real harmony, sublime, nirvana

My soul does *ache*

Isolation – Empty – Quiet – Monotony – Ache – Silence – Longing –
Seclusion

WRITE A POEM ABOUT

Possibilities

Human evolution

Limitless potential

Kinetic energy, *action* now

Specific measurable goals with realistic deadlines

Guarantee of death

The bucket list

A *promise* kept

One life to live

Third-eye *foresight*

Artificial intelligence inevitable takeover

Plausible hazard, shot at the local bodega

An accident waiting to happen

Self-fulfilling prophecy

Munchausen by proxy

Transference, Stockholm syndrome

Manipulated by propaganda

Hypnotized by subliminal messages

Restrict freedom, call it protection

Redefine the line between good and evil

The gray Jedi

Future securities

Gather the world's resources

Defend it with nuclear weapons

Medicate the masses

Individual quest to decimate the system

Imagine a better world

Manage my immediate habits

In order to save the children

Start with the man in the mirror

Potential – Limitless – Foresight – Promise – Action – Hazard – Plausible – Shot

WRITE A POEM ABOUT

Values

All thoughts are relevant

But can be dismissed

The mind sows the seeds it's planted

Vulgar, inappropriate

The evil is so prevalent

I stay positive

I am raising my *standards*

Using my passion

Never watch porn or imagine infidelity

Code of *ethics*

The *mores* of a Christian household

Super *conscience* of my place in the world

A duty to build the culture

Evolution, generations, pure students

Put myself through the *scruples* so that we can all grow

Future *ideals*, present *tenet*

Everything in balance

Fight the fear

Establish better habits

How we treat, eat, speak, lead

Live by a set of values

Forgive myself for my failures

Awareness of expectation

Acting as if, then becoming

Born, raised, made man

Mores – Scruples – Ethics – Standards – Conscience – Ideals – Code – Tenet

WRITE A POEM ABOUT

Snow

Desire the dance

I liked the *white* a lot

On the back of a CD case cracks caught crumbs

Lick the glass, cut my tongue

The index captures every last *flake*

Spread it all over the gums

Roll up a dollar bill

Use an id to divide the lines

Giant boulders, no pencils

Be careful the bump *drifts*

Inhale in a *flurry*

Nostrils absorb fresh powder

To toot my horn, I got the best

Pure, expensive, crystal candy

My best friend is El Salvadorean

Past shady barters acquaintance beef

Scary street strangers sharing numb teeth

Super small plastic baggies twist and tie to close

Wig froze, heart pounding, head rush

Motor mouth chattering, face red, eyes flushed

Love *hush*, car *frost*, windows fogged

Outside *blizzard* completely ignored

Timid touch, clammy palm, dry taste

Laying in the snow, attempting to be an angel

Acting *chill* as the chills go up and down my spine

We are finally alone

We talked all night

White – Drifts – Hush – Chill – Flurry – Blizzard – Flake – Frost

WRITE A POEM ABOUT

Creativity

Inventive for incentive

Please purchase my book

Your dollar is very valuable

Evaluate how you spend

Clever negotiator, a *genius*, enough to affirm myself every day

Talent without discipline, another has-been

Inexplicable, immaculate *imagination*

Turn profit engineer terraform

Xerox oxygen, code storms

Illuminati Hurricane Helene Carolina

Destroy homes, resource quartz

Eliminate *inspiration*, equal basic income

Erase raises, penciled out pensions, no social security left

Taxed on what you make, taxed on what you spend, taxed on the land

Inflation equaling the amount the Fed wants circling

Scam calls, texts, and spam emails

We let Google track every step we take on the internet

They use that to record every move we make on the planet

Brainwash our thoughts, TikTok the algorithm

A.I. the art, digitalized Robin Wright

Congress stopped progress

True *originality* is demolished

They killed the inventor of the renewable energy battery

Murdered Tupac and Biggie, did he P. Diddy?

Power, money, respect

A stolen *vision*, the deleted witness kept quiet

Survival by any means necessary

Illumination, creation elimination

The best way to control evolution

Destroy to rebuild

Inventive – Originality – Talent – Vision – Clever – Imagination – Genius –
Inspiration

WRITE A POEM ABOUT

Weakness

The court judged me as delinquent as a minor

Ordered medication, a *folly*

Ritalin didn't fix me

In high school, my girlfriend got a restraining order

As an adult, in therapy, and anger management

Height short, weight thin, small man complex, big bravado

No father to teach discipline

Abusive household

Secret sex

Molestation *debility*

Trained *frailty*

Ingrained trauma, forever *shortcoming*

Lack of love

I had to switch the narrative

Fix the voice in my head

Survivor, not a *feeble* victim

Say affirmations, neurolinguistic programming

Change my stars, trade in the cards I was dealt

Ask for help

Flip the *vice* from television to seeking wisdom

Reading books, making good decisions

The old *vulnerability* is now a power

Tragedy turned into triumph

Harder, better, faster, stronger

My weakness was the identity I had of myself

Because of what happened to me

The weakness was the identity I had of myself

Now it's my ultimate strength

Debility – Frailty – Lack – Folly – Vice – Shortcoming – Feeble -
Vulnerability

WRITE A POEM ABOUT

Cowardice

There has been a constant problem

I am not stoic

I am open to suggestion

So many *weak* words imprinted

Fake friends that wanted my detriment

Who's jealous of who

Timid toward the pretty girl

Afraid she could see my facade

No muscles, no confidence

I am *spineless*, a complete *wimp*, scrawny, puny

I put my head down, he swoops in taking advantage

Manipulating, pressuring

The *object* of my affection

He's now smashing

I feel extra *pathetic*

I congratulate him when he starts bragging

Self-worth displaced again

Deserter of goals

Depressed, alone

Cocooned in bed, dessert eating

The worst thing is touching yourself

Satisfying urges surfing the internet

The damage done by cowardice can affect every aspect of self

The world needs strong leaders

WRITE A POEM ABOUT

Luck

Daily doses of ferocious awesomeness

A *stroke* of genius how I spoke so authentic

To no *avail*, I am still misunderstood

I want *fortune*

I will take fame

If I lose, there's no one to blame

When I *win* it's only a game

Live or die

It's all the same

After all, they can only hang you once

Pick the *odds*

100% jackpot

Break the bank

Side hustle, moth to the flame

Baby needs new pair of shoes

Go for *profit*

Desire the competition

The *windfall* of women

No longer, I'm married

I've carried this burden of expectation

Potential for greatness

Burning motivation and wasted it

Today I make my declaration

I am an amazing individual

Saying affirmations, practicing meditations

Attempting to believe in myself

I am lucky I survived the tragedies of my youth

I got over being a victim

I learned the truth

Luck won't give me a million dollars

But having luck on my side may bring my closer

Stroke – Profit – Win – Windfall – Break – Avail – Odds – Fortune

WRITE A POEM ABOUT

Sadness

I dwelled in sadness for a long time

Depression was my best friend

Like a *despondent* roommate, he let me do nothing

Collect unemployment checks

Apathy becomes comforting

Luckily God found me

I was like whoa *woe*, I don't need *sorrow*

Jesus died for my *suffering*

He arose from the dead and so can I

Cannot feel *grief* for my former self

Replace *bleakness* with euphoria

Erase the *dysphoria* of weakness

Gain strength from gratitude

For every day I am alive I can grow

Optimistic attitude never wavers, glass half full

Hard to break habits

Turned *heartache* into attachment

Combined passions to confidence

My experience and beliefs graph my identity

Craft my soul, a clay sculpture God is forever forming

Prince charming washed by earth dirt

The sadness, a cocooned caterpillar

Inner beauty a butterfly

Heartache – Bleakness – Dysphoria – Woe – Grief – Despondent – Sorrow –
Suffering

WRITE A POEM ABOUT

Compassion

Introspection, a trip into my feelings

Barbequed *benevolence*

Pittsburgh charred *heart*

The Archdiocese of Chicago passing out hot meals

Receive *clemency* repenting, praying

Women do get weary, show a little *tenderness*

Jesus forgives, live Christian ethics

Bitter faith, gritty faith

Here there is all fear, no honor

We walk around the man lying on the ground

Fight wars for more oil control

Won't help the homeless, can't feed the *meek*

House criminals, give government funds to immigrants

I know human compassion is limited

But I fear we are not exhibiting it

Enhance *empathy* instead of growing atrophy

Asking to act against apathy

The Maine state of mind is hunting

Pampas acts show no *mercy* to weaker creatures

Roadkill rally, from friends to funerals

Love doesn't always follow usual paths

Our choices as individuals matter in the grand scheme of all things

Balance strength and compassion

The Neo-Human evolution

Perfect physical, spiritual specimen, chiseled

Softness is like the Q-Tip, clears the edges, helps you hear better and feel better

Kindness connecting a couple of strangers

After years, after displaced decades

In Heaven, our souls are fulfilled forever

Stop hoarding, give yourself and your stuff away

Our purpose is to pass on

Benevolence – Meek – Tenderness – Empathy – Heart – Clemency – Mercy – Softness

WRITE A POEM ABOUT

Soul Mate

It didn't take long. I knew it right away

I saw it your pictures, we are *kindred* spirits

A genuine smile, inner beauty with green hair

Attractive body, eventual *lover*, my forever *partner*

A prayer, you would see

I could be, a good a *companion*

Instantly you made me feel like the man

You told me not to stop with the compliments

You were made beautiful, feel beautiful

I believe I projected us

I manifested you, my wife into my life

At the same time, you believe you projected me, your *spouse*, and our house

We are each other's *confidante*

We had a large wedding, and also a Covid one

2 anniversaries, we love each other twice as much

I wrote "This Love" at the start

More than a crush

Through harsh cold we walk

Tundra without my *sweetheart*

Warm you up with kind words while out in the elements

This is *true love*

Marrwwidge that blessed arrangement

Till' death do us part

The Universe has a purpose for us

Guided and protected by angels

We shape our destiny, create our fate

Choose love, choose respect

I choose you forever

Hannah, you are my eternal soul mate

Partner – Lover – Spouse – Kindred – Confidante – Companion - True Love
– Sweetheart

WRITE A POEM ABOUT

Perspective

The pessimist half empty

The optimist half full

Positive affirmations

Negative self-talk

Conditioned programming

Robot monkeys

New instincts, automatic reactions

Muscle memory

Senses, smells, balance, *context*

Neural chemical manipulation

Images, sounds

Subliminal messages

White men can't jump

Immigrant murderers

Frame of mind- stuck

Liberal left, radical right

TikTok the clock likes subscribers

Hit the *angle* insta

Viewpoint vista

Sunshine and rainbows

California dreaming

Hoops, wall street, crack rock

Broad options

Venice beach *scene*

Boardwalk, point place

Money monopoly, paradigm *shift*

Alternate dimension, manifest miracles, mirrored identity

Vast ocean, unlimited universe

The wicked witch stole the red slippers

Glass was given to Cinderella

I do feel good about myself

I should

Viewpoint – Context – Scene – Vista – Shift – Frame – Broad – Angle

WRITE A POEM ABOUT

Wishes

The *intention* is acquisitions

Money, power, respect

Fame is an *ambition* of vanity

An *aspiration* of envy

My *yearning* has altered

No more dares like I don't care

Responsible for more than myself

My *desire* is simple

Financial security for my family

Earning recognition for the results from *will* power

A creative appreciation

Erasing incredibly stupid decisions

Fixing broken records

Time does not help the *longing*

3000 years of wishing

Humbly kneeling, rubbing lamps, scratching tickets

Hope does not want

She believes it can be done

No more wishes before bedtime

Bluetooth playing frequencies

528, 963, 741

Sacred geometry, gut cleansing, gratitude

God already granted me everything I will ever need

Health, run, don't think, grab shoes

I stash them next to the bed

Intention – Aspiration – Ambition – Hope – Longing – Will – Yearning –
Desire

WRITE A POEM ABOUT

Warmth

She asked me to send money

To Accra, Ghana Africa

Her name was *Comfort*

Catfish yahoo online chat room

A fool for love

I was craving *affection*

Settled for attention

Someone who would listen, show *reassurance*

My lonely heart desperate for *closeness*

She said she was a friend of my cousin

And that we had already met

At a pool party, I mentioned something about her aura

Was it a pond/lake, she couldn't be sure

It wasn't the first lie she tried to deny

Piles high I let slide, against my better judgement

I kept up the charade

Asked for her phone number and got 12 digits

Plus 3,2 in front of it

Confused I demanded *sharing* a real pic right now

I thought she lived down state, not half-way across the planet

The tone on the phone, not near my home

When we first spoke, E.T., extra *tenderness*, easy texts

Miscommunication, manipulation, mislead emotions

Her picture, a model, the bait

She posted fake photos, bathing suits

The hotness did *radiate*

It had felt great to have an online date, every day

It got to be, I couldn't wait until I got that ping notification

Anxious to speak to the person, who turned out to be foreign

I knew it was too good to be true

The warmth of comfort

It's cold to know the *glow* was evil

Eventually, she asked for some cash

I figure I wasn't her first victim

Comfort – Tenderness – Sharing – Closeness – Reassurance – Glow – Affection
– Radiate

WRITE A POEM ABOUT

Spring

No spring in my step today

An initial burst then I'm dead tired

Running the hamster wheel

After a nap, *fresh*

Vernal, seedtime

New *beginnings*, new ideas

Contemplating purpose

The *primrose budding*

A *perennial* plant blooming

Sunshine, rain, joy and pain

Seasons change and so do I

Flowering capturing precipitation

Cell osmosis, adaptive nuclei

Simple energy transformation

Eat nutrients planted in the soil

Fruits, vegetables, purchased at the local grocery store

A nomadic lifestyle evolved

Woke emotional intelligence

Trees breathe CO_2 and exhale oxygen

We destroy the jungle

Mother Nature Oedipus complex

Human evolution

Technical progress

The Universe has a purpose

And, so do I

Spread the good message

Eloquently describe the vibe

In the form of wicked cool spoken word lyrics

Spring forward

Never fall back

Budding – Flowering – Vernal – Seedtime – Beginnings – Fresh – Perennial –
Primrose

WRITE A POEM ABOUT

Regret

Regrets form shame
Penitence or blame
Depressed, *repine* about life
Find comfort
Excuses for *bitterness*
Lament in the lack of action
Hide under covers
No face in public
Self-reproach against our own better judgement
Torn ego, no talent
To *bemoan* one's own fate
Rue any assistance
Time is too late
Quit admit *defeat*
Feeling weak
Starting next week
One day I will
Tomorrow I will start or tomorrow I will quit that addiction
A new year, a new choice
Let that old voice control
Or affirm positive statements
Regret or embrace change

Penitence – Self-reproach – Repine – Bitterness – Lament – Bemoan – Rue –
Defeat

WRITE A POEM ABOUT

Silence

After laughter comes tears

We miss the departed

Gangsters don't die they multiply

A real g is silent, like in lasagna

The loudest statement can come from a *whisper*

Practice *stillness* release tension

Position posture, prepare a mental picture

Breath for *calm*

Intention to halt the heart to a slow *lull*

Make believe imagination memories come and go

Meditation to *hush* the noise

The truth is uncovered

Know thy self, bend the spoon

Use *quietude* to boost inner *peace*

Mirror the images on the mental screen

Become the person in the vision

Neo-thinking *profound* understanding

The key to getting what you want

Stop wanting, don't say anything

Become the one who is expecting

Hush – Lull – Peace – Calm – Quietude – Stillness – Whisper – Profound

WRITE A POEM ABOUT

Growing Older

Current active behavior geared towards the *golden years*

Retirement funds, Roth IRA, 401K

A diversified portfolio

Comfort in my *dotage*

Never *decline* on credit

In my youth, I was stupid

In my prime, I'm wiser, more *mature*

Able to decipher nonsense quicker

Using extraordinary wit, shoot from the hip

Rebuttal anything, yo-mama jokes

8-mile battles

We became a *venerable* generation

Lead the vulnerable away from constant manipulation

Committed practical embarrassments

Depantsing, food fights, whoopie cushions

Attempted to have the rules *perfected*

No mass shootings

Revenge of the nerds

Step up get served

We followed traditions

Evolved resolve changed what was important

Legalized marijuana

X, Millennials to Z

I-Pad babies become internet celebrities

Young punks thank the old farts

They created it

Have honor, respect your elder

I, aye captain

Golden Years – Mature – Dotage – Decline – Elder – Venerable – Evolved –
Perfected

WRITE A POEM ABOUT

Visions

Insight into *brilliance*

Your first million

Followed the *acumen* of successful men

Read the book, accumulated knowledge

Positive mindset, mirror theory, highly effective habits

The Art of War, Money: Master the Game

Value the *perception*

Miracles don't just happen. You have to believe they will

Imagination before *musings*

The *fancies* of an unlimited being

Create whatever we want to be

See, in our heads, first

Reality manifests images hard wired from our mother's eyes

A *glimpse* into the future

The baby's self-awareness of its own reflection

We can only nurture, nature designs

I didn't allow time to pass

Without examining the experience

I saw I could fill each moment of my life

To the fullest; with love

Let God mold the soul

His vision is my destiny

Perception – Glimpse – Insight – Acumen – Brilliance – Fancies – Musings –
Imagination

WRITE A POEM ABOUT

Travel

People, places, things

Adventures, journeys, experiences

Touring the world

An *expedition* through Earth

As I take the *trek*

He is beside me

When the sea is at its most depth

Only one footprint can be seen in the sand

A fantastic *voyage*, life

Short *trip* to a visceral destination

A spirit to *tour* the universe

My authentic-self *wandering*

Through actualized imagination

Perception born

A *ramble* back to Heaven

Trek – Ramble – Wandering – Touring – Expedition – Tour – Voyage – Trip

WRITE A POEM ABOUT

A Voyage

Harder to start than finish

Just do it

All day, I dream about sports

Strategies, metaphors for courage

Team and individual goals

The *journey* to the end zone

Daunting to *jaunt* ten yards

Small steps, practice the basics

Assists *passage* through the defense

Crossing the bridge of adversity into maturity

Swing at the first pitch, curveball

You miss 100% of the shots you don't take

Winning, losing, rain delays

Handling the pressure, *discovery* of willpower

Exposing the full potential of our talents

Explore for more potential talent

Encouragement, dealing with defeat

Failure and resilience

Penalties for breaking the rules

The universal *search* for truth

The uniform, the *vessel*, the body, the temple

Pushed past limits, exquisite performance

The art of the dunk

Catching the Hail Mary pass

Winning the championship

WRITE A POEM ABOUT

Trust

Am I doing too much?

Am I doing enough?

Power dictates

Time to take *charge* of this life

Negotiate from higher leverage

Manipulate the environment

The loser is a victim

Alive during the great depression

Alive during a zombie apocalypse

Look at the streets of San Fransisco

An epidemic of sickness, addiction

Take *stock* in your blessings

For every day I am grateful

More *conviction* to achieve my goals

We are *steadfast* for change

Give *credence* to hope

Let go of the choice, the answer is obvious

Trust yourself

Energy is consumed, transformed, exerted, and recycled

Potential converted to kinetic

Recuperation, day and night, dark and light cycles

Spinning *loyal* to speed, size, and mass

Consistent *integrity*, gravity of intention

The universe equation will never be solvable

Einstein only had a theory

Our questions can move mountains

Our imaginations can build skyscrapers

Are we *sure* we are going in the right direction?

Each individual must trust himself

It's not in my understanding to make your decisions

Follow the money, find the power in the world

Either trust it or fight the system

Stock – Sure – Credence – Conviction – Loyal – Integrity – Charge –
Steadfast

WRITE A POEM ABOUT

Broken Heart

Khaki pants

Long sleeves

Wife beater

Man city

Tiki taka

Tinder tender

Achy breaky

Chicken *stricken*

Vulnerable venerable

Doleful soulful

2pac *pain*

Nas momma

Last dance

Jordan goat

Broken curse

Tyson Paul

Friday night

Heartsick rock

Alone bedroom

Brother *betrayal*

Forget *regret*

Blame game

Red flag

Throw pillow

Ring toss

Dream girl

Fear blonde

Alicia *crushed*

Batman sucks

Robin egg

Exposed elements

Hunger snow

Inner child

Elephant room

Wish fulfilled

Destiny manifest

Spouse father

Worry confidence

A mulatto an albino

A mosquito my libido

Nirvana dumb

Ignorance bliss

Broken heart

Have faith

Trust God

The End

Stricken – Heartsick – Pain – Doleful – Betrayal – Vulnerable – Crushed –
Regret

WRITE A POEM ABOUT

Poetry

I don't feel like writing poetry today

No urge to *rhyme*

No *verse* chorus verse in my mind

I am anti-*stanza* this evening

This *composition* has no *muse*

Dancing without *rhythm*

The iambic pentameter is off

Inside the box thinking

The cat's out the bag

Dead or alive

An *epic* metaphor is not needed

Invisible sweat

Value the effort

Complete the agenda

Ending *lyric* abrupt

Verse – Rhyme – Stanza – Composition – Muse – Rhythm – Lyric – Epic

WRITE A POEM ABOUT

Fame

Fame *renown*

I own my lack there of

I had *popularity* in school

Until I moved

I couldn't bring along my *reputation*

Acted out to get noticed

Like Willie Olsen punished *standing* in the corner

The class clown isn't stupid

Every person covets *acknowledgement*

Inclusion is a hell of a drug

I did things that were *immoral* to appear normal

Having good *repute* meant stomping on others wearing boots

Driven to be accepted

Applauding a man that slapped another man in the face

Jealousy and intimidation

Peer-pressure measured by clicks

Likes, subscribers, viewing minutes

Arguments in the comments boost the algorithm

No *regard* for freedom of other's opinions

Judge harshly rule the system

Manipulate with a fallacy prophecy

The huge notion to be enormously famous

Hopeless, a pipe dream

We used to get 15 minutes

Now all these kids need is

It seems anyone will do just about anything for

10 seconds of fame

*Renown – Repute – Standing – Acknowledgement – Reputation – Popularity
– Regard – Immoral*

Imperfection

My interpretation of imperfection

Use all the words, say all the sentences

It makes it simple

Uniqueness is my directive

We have the blueprint

Explain definition of the derivative

No one is perfect

I copy, bite, sample

Be *foible* in my poetry

In *nature,* find comfort

The *defect,* by default conserve energy

No originality in art

Everything's turned pop

Flip the image

Negatives become positives

Repackaged, the *blemish* gets covered up

The news never stops

Following the trends

Accountability looked at like arrogance

Forget the *shortcoming*

Cancelled, blackballed from the group

Marred by letting it occur for so long

We can all change a *flaw*

We can become more than we are

The imperfection is that we don't all aim for perfection

Attention collection rather than substance

And in that way our evolution loses

Every Christmas we watch a different version of a Christmas
Carol/Scrooge

They are always asking me for more like

A bullet with butterfly wings

*Flaw – Uniqueness – Foible – Blemish – Shortcoming – Nature – Defect –
Marred*

WRITE A POEM ABOUT

A Work of Art

In the beginning

Bang- fertilization

From egg to embryo

Formulization of the universe

Cells grow, die, multiply

Mitochondria forms, uses nutrients

The origin of species

Lightning hits organic ooze

Animals poop soil

Petrology caves, mines *craft* mountains

Plationic shifts

Portrait at 6 months

65 million years

Dinosaurs on t-shirts

Landscape mobile hanging overhead

Night *light* birds flying away

Graffiti spray paint

Ninja *brushstrokes*, death grip

Crayons of every *color*

Every silver linings got a touch of grey

Texture the *shade*

Rainbows with glitter polka dot sequence

The name is displayed everywhere

Respect is earned

A clean slate dirtied or nurtured

A child's choices determine his destiny

Born pure, finite resources

In order to build you have to destroy

The missile through the abdomen expands the stomach

Visit the monument

Hold the precious baby securely

Portrait – Brushstrokes – Texture – Color – Craft – Landscape – Shade – Light

WRITE A POEM ABOUT

Moments

I heard there are tunnels under L.A.

It lets the Hollywood elite escape traffic

Quick exits at the next studio or stadium

They even have gas stations and Starbucks

But the stars don't pay no bucks

Isolation out of touch

White *privilege* switched to rich privilege

Walls and gates to expand the *difference*

The *injustice* was built up around us

Judicial *bias* based on tiredness

Get a lighter sentence when the case is heard earlier in the day

Afford a good lawyer who dug up dirt on the State's attorney

Systematic *racism*, more opportunities in my resumé

All I know is, when I was arrested it could have been way worse

Disparity in the numbers

Percentage of blacks imprisoned

Imagine being chased, captured and then lynched

Especially because you knew how to do business

You took money out another man's pocket

Being educated gets you hunted

They keep their secrets from being discovered

The illuminati will never illuminate how to attain and maintain a fortune

School teaches obedience

Born under *misfortune*

Swear its *unfair* political activist

In the zeitgeist we are all zombies

WRITE A POEM ABOUT

A Shadow

Start a shadow from the end, work backwards. Distinctive tricks *extinguish* goals, conquer personal problems. *Obscure* even more, no now, bright future. The doubt, no, *obfuscate* others. *Two-faced*, sinner, Sith, *dark side*, *lightless*, unable to *mimic*. I'm limitless, original, confident, awesome. Positive talk, thoughts bad, *blacken* clouds cover, exposed sunshine, happiness, fixed world.

World fixed, happiness, sunshine exposed. Cover clouds blacken bad thoughts. Talk positive, awesome, confident, original, limitless I'm. Mimic to unable. Lightless, dark side, Sith, sinner, two-faced others obfuscate. No doubt the future bright now. No more even obscure problems. Personal conquer goals, extinguish tricks distinctive. Backwards work, end the, from shadow, a start.

Two-faced - Dark side – Lightless – Mimic – Obfuscate – Blacken – Obscure – Extinguish

www.ingramcontent.com/pod-product-compliance
Lightning Source LLC
Chambersburg PA
CBHW051151120626
46547CB00012B/1039